MEL BAY'S

ELECTRI BLUES GUITAR WORKOUT

BY DAN BOWDEN

1 2 3 4 5 6 7 8 9 0

Visit us on the Web at www.melbay.com — E-mail us at email@melbay.com

Table of Contents

Pentatonic Minor Scale/Key of A

Memorize this basic fingering.

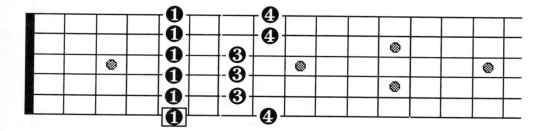

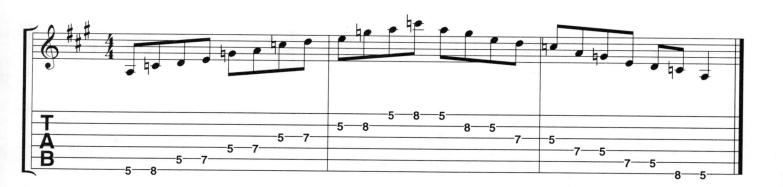

Right Hand Picking Exercises

Practice with a steady tempo observing pick direction markings.

 = Down-stroke

V = Up-stroke

QUARTER NOTES

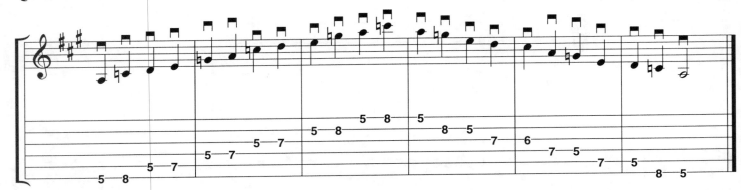

EIGHT NOTES

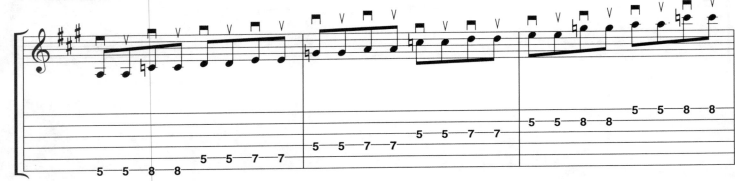

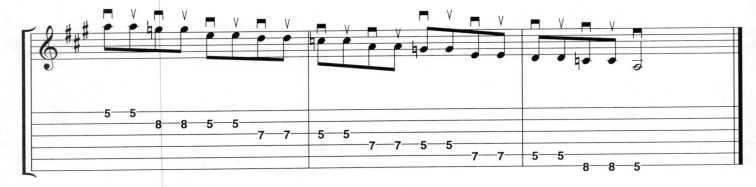

SWING EIGHT NOTES

TRIPLETS

SIXTEENTH NOTES

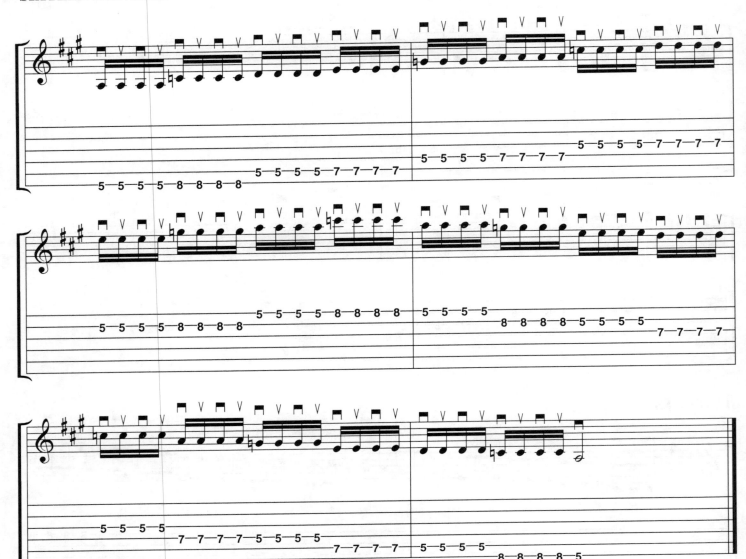

Pentatonic Scale Sequence Patterns

The next five examples are sequence patterns applied to the A pentatonic minor scale.

EXAMPLE 1

EXAMPLE 2

EXAMPLE 3

EXAMPLE 4

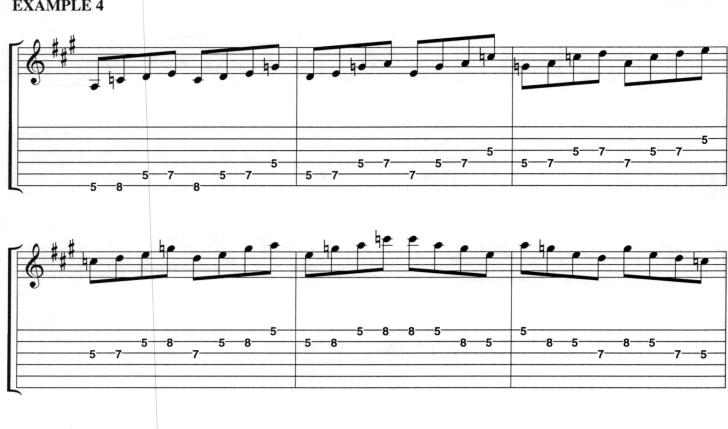

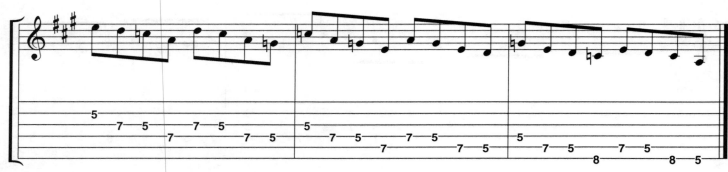

EXAMPLE 5

Minor Blues Scale/Key of A

Memorize this basic fingering.

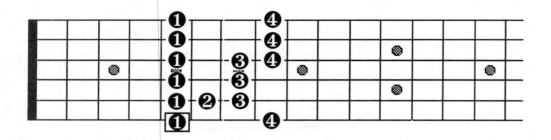

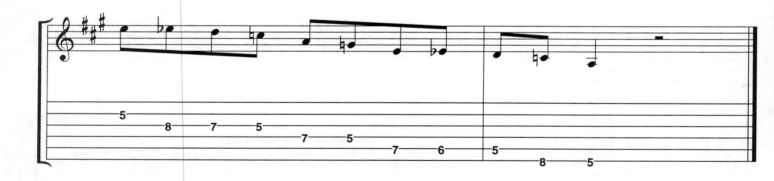

Minor Blues Scale
Sequence Patterns

The next five examples are sequence patterns applied to the A pentatonic minor scale.

EXAMPLE 6

EXAMPLE 7

14

EXAMPLE 8

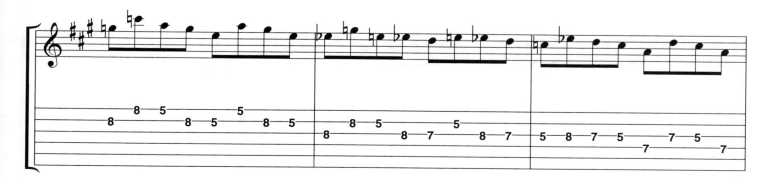

15

EXAMPLE 9

Hammer-ons and Pull-offs

Pick only the first note of each two–note grouping that is connected with a slur (⌢) for smoother phrasing and to strengthen the left-hand fingers.

EXAMPLE 10

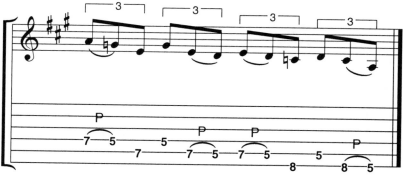

EXAMPLE 11

18

EXAMPLE 12

EXAMPLE 13

EXAMPLE 14

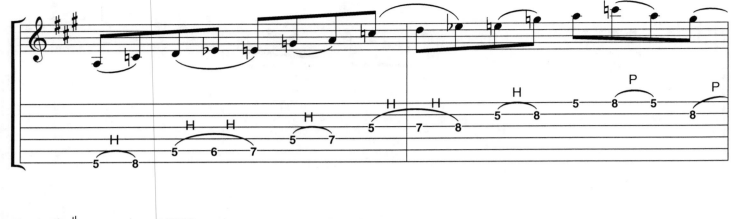

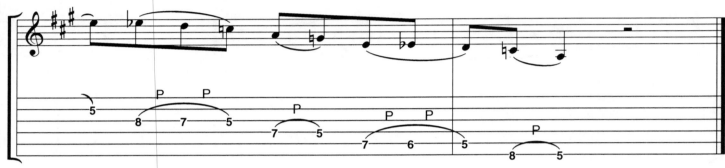

* There are some three-note slurred groupings in example 14.

Double-stops

Double-stops are two notes played simultaneously. These are commonly used in blues and 50's style rock solos.

Sixths

Sixths are double-stops that are an interval of a sixth apart. They are common in turnarounds.

1/4 Step Bends

A slight string bend with the 3rd or 4th finger.

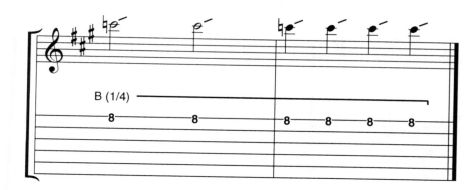

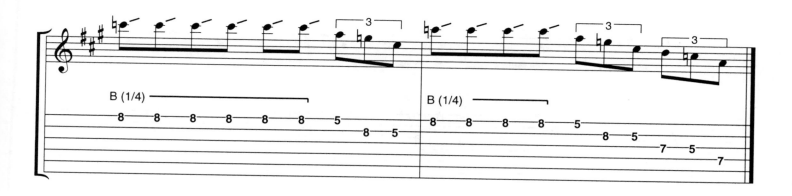

1/2 Step Bends

With the third finger, push the 3rd string up to match the note that sounds one fret above.

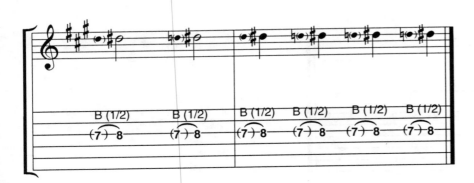

Whole-step bends/3rd string

With the third finger, push the third string up to match the note that sounds two frets above.

Whole-step bends/2nd string

With the third finger, push the second string up to match the note that sounds two frets above.

Whole-step bends/1st string

With the third finger, push the first string up to match the note that sounds two frets above.

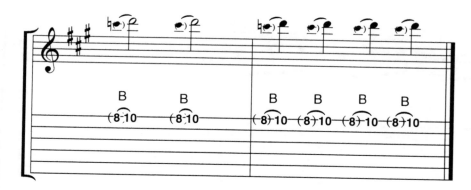

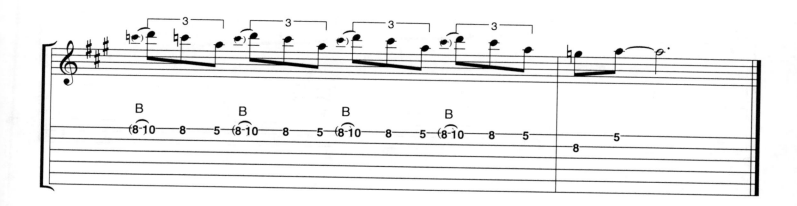

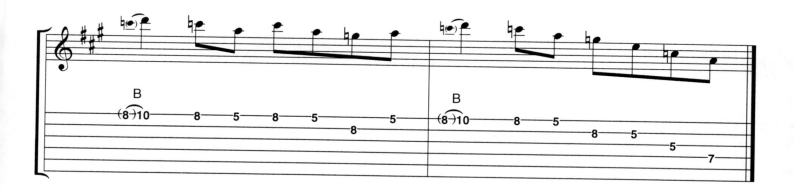

Bend–Release

After bending to the desired pitch, relax the string back to the unbent position.

Pentatonic Minor Scales
5 Fingerings/Key of A

Learn all scale fingerings for soloing over the entire fretboard.

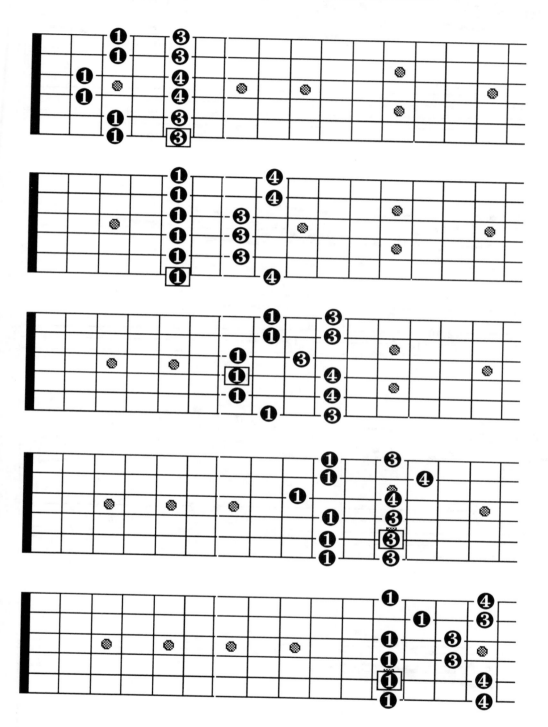

Connecting the 5 Pentatonic Minor Fingerings

Change fretboard position on the 1st and 6th strings.

Minor Blues Scales
5 Fingerings/Key of A

Learn all scale fingerings for soloing over the entire fretboard.

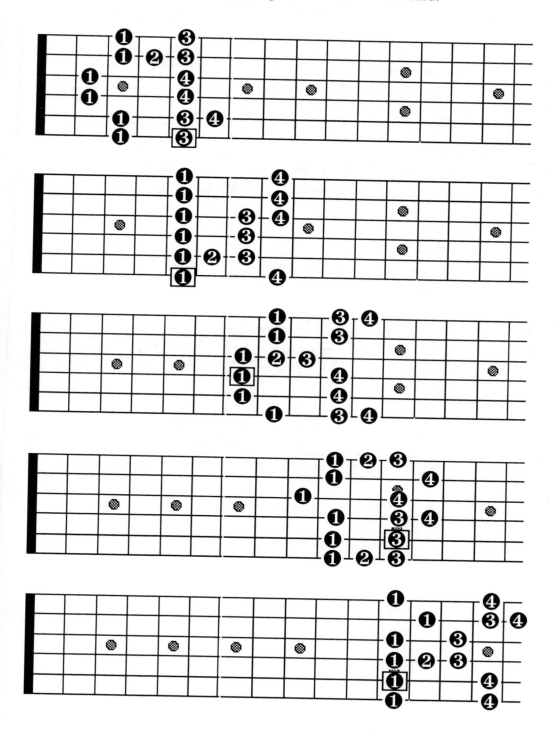

Connecting the 5 Minor Blues Scale Fingerings

Change fretboard position on the 1st and 6th strings.

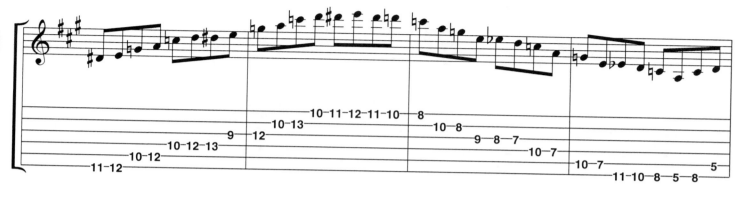

Pentatonic Major Scales
5 Fingerings/Key of A

Memorize and apply all sequence patterns from pentatonic minor examples.

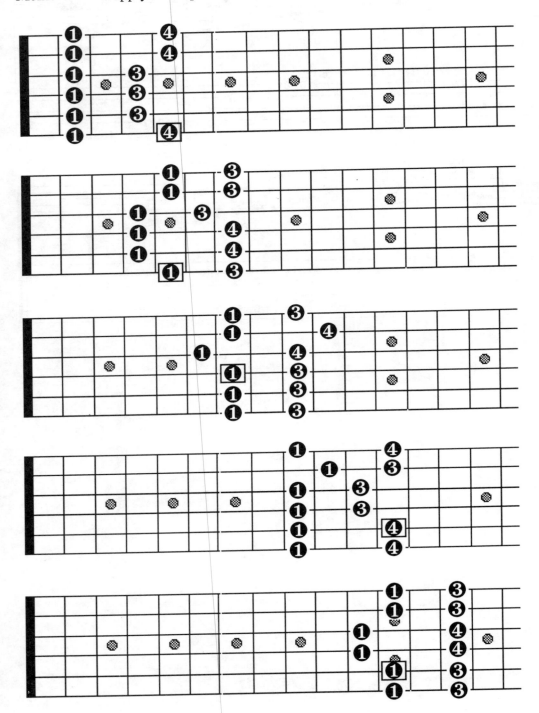

Major Blues Scales
5 Fingerings/Key of A

Memorize and apply all sequence patterns from minor blues scale examples.

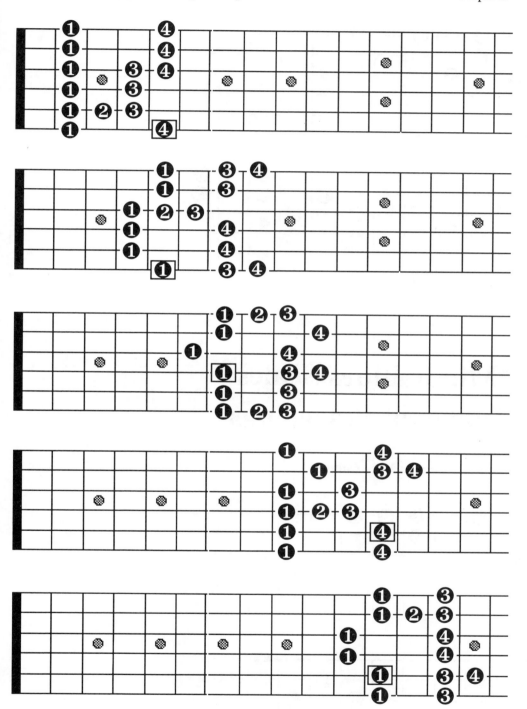

Pentatonic Minor Scales
Diagonal Fingerings

Memorize and apply all sequence patterns from earlier examples.

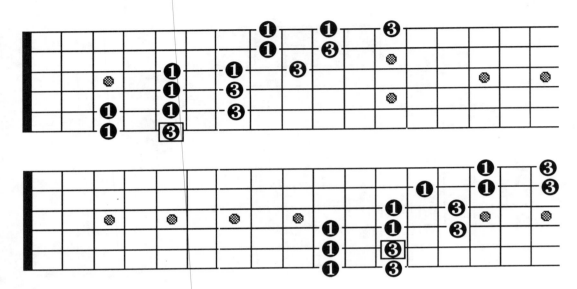

Minor Blues Scales
Diagonal Fingerings

Memorize and apply all sequence patterns from earlier examples.

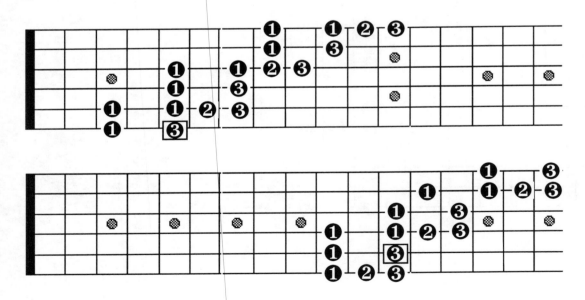

Seventh Chord Arpeggio
Fingerings

Arpeggios are comprised of the notes that make up chords. It's important to learn to solo with chord tones as well as scales. Memorize the forms below and practice soloing on a 12 Bar progression (key of A), emphasizing the notes of each individual chord: I (A7) IV (D7) V (E7)

A7 Arpeggio

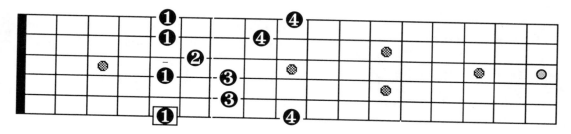

D7 Arpeggio

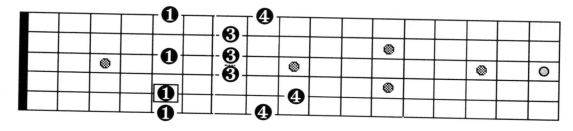

E7 Arpeggio

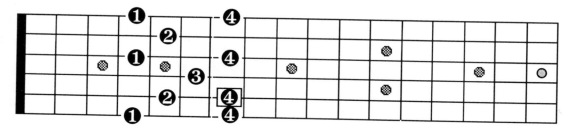

Dan Bowden

Dan Bowden is a guitarist with roots running deep in the blues, jazz, and rock genres. He currently records and performs with the Boston based group, Stingy Brimm. Dan has authored a number of guitar transcription books for Mel Bay Publications that encompass jazz, electric blues, country blues, slide guitar, finger-style acoustic guitar, and bluegrass. He is also the author of Mel Bay's *Complete Accompaniment Method for Guitar* (MB#98688BCD). Dan has been a faculty member at Berklee College of Music in Boston, Ma. since 1989.